# La'Sandra:
# The Christian,
# The Woman,
# The Cosmetologist

## Keys on surviving the Beauty Beast

La'Sandra: The Christian, The Woman,
The Cosmetologist
Keys on surviving the Beauty Beast

Authored by La'Sandra Easley
Edited by La'Sandra Easley

Special thanks to:

La'Sandra's Hair Stylist for the book cover

Sadie "Chipi" Wilson

La'Sandra's Nail Tech Artist for the book cover

Janine Crump

Published by La'Sandra Easley

Published 2015

A Beauty Bar

P.R.O
Professional Resource Org.

First Printing: 2015

ISBN: 978-1-329-56702-3

Published by New Anointing Press

www.provizion.org

To order additional books by La'Sandra Easley go to lulu.com or email her directly at pro1vizion@gmail.com.  For additional services provided by Professional Resource Organization log on to www.provizion.org.

# Dedication

I dedicate this work, my years of experience, the ups, downs, going through and coming through to every person that has and has not been discovered or acknowledged for their work and talents in the Beauty insdustry which I lovingly nicknamed **"The Beauty Beast."** Nothing shows you what you're made of like going after what you love. From one P.R.O to another…don't ever give up! If you're in a place of learning new things and you have dreams, don't give up. If you've been in the field for over 10 years and think you hit a dead end…don't give up. I hope this book encourages you to pursue your passion because this was my reason for writing it.

Had I not gone through what I'v been through I'd have nothing to write about.

You need to read this book because smart people learn from their own mistakes but wise people learn from the mistakes of others. I pray you remain open minded as you read this book because I am as authenitc in telling the truth about my career and its various battles. Some things I went throuh in my career I wouldn't wish on my worst enemy! Some things I went through was because I put myself through a lot of things unnecessarily! All in all I hope this book makes you laugh, think and feel challenegd because everything I've achieved was because God is with me just like He is with you!

God bless!

# Table of contents

# Acknowledgements

Jesus Christ is not a style for me. I don't acknowledge Him because it's the right thing to do. I acknowledge Who I live for and love. He is my lifestyle. He has never failed me or left me disappointed...ever! All my love, praise, life, every area in my life belongs to Jesus Christ!

To my loving parents...I don't have enough of an adequate language to express my love and gratitude to for your support. Thank you for not judging me when I lost jobs, wanted to move locations or in anything I did you've always supported me and been there consistently.

Bishop Anthony and Lady Yvonne Willis- like my biological parents you've always supported everything I've done as far as ministry. Bishop thank you for pushing me when I was in college; you would not let me settle for anything less than excellence! Thank you!

To Stephanie, Angela, Dr. Thompson and the rest of the Nabi'Im Council, thank you for your prayers and encouragement concerning this book! It was a labor of love and you all pushed me through it. Thank you!

To everyone that guided me through my career be your contribution positive or negative, God used it for His Glory! Thank you!

# Where it all began…

## Proverbs 18:16

### A man's gift makes room for him and brings him before great men

I was in high school in Vallejo California my sophomore year and I had a discussion with my father whom is also my best friend. "Well girl what are you going to do with your life?" He asked while we were having breakfast out. "Your school is willing to certify you through the state to do hair or work on computers and neither of those fields are going anywhere, which one are you going to do?"

I thought to myself naturally beauty felt like a good fit. I was sixteen years old and I never imagined the gifts God had given me would cause me to travel and see the world, be a home owner, car owner, own my own product line for bath, body and skincare for men and women.

I never imagined I would be a Barber, I just wanted to do hair but I got a buzz and a thrill the first time I held a pair of Wahl clippers and the betrayal I felt every time I dropped one of those little money makers! I never imagined hair could ever be my ministry.

Please don't mistake me for a fairytale career woman because I am not! My story is my gut brutal honest story of mistakes I made, my self-discoveries and situations I should never have been in that stunted my growth professionally as well as spiritually. I struggled with staying saved and balancing my faith as well as making money.

It was during that time I heard God call my name. I don't know how I knew I just "Knew". My Father wanted me to fulfill my purpose in Him and I didn't have one detail but I felt the need to go to church and I found an old school Baptist church. Some people from my high school also attended there…No one could answer my questions. How do I get saved? How do I know God is calling me? Will someone teach me how I should pray? Why is the Bible so big and how do I read it? I joined the choir thinking it would somehow bring me closer to the The Lord God Jehovah but no. Singing helped me express my love to God but being in the choir just gave me a better view of the pulpit. It wasn't enough. Something in me wanted and craved more.

When I would read the bible I wanted to know this Jesus that walks on water and is a friend. He intrigued me. I didn't know what I was reading but it was "right", I don't know how it was right but it was and still is to me today. Looking back I don't think I would still be here if God had not gotten a hold of me back then.

I really suffered with identity struggles as well as low self-esteem. At the time I was a BBW (Beautiful Big or Black Woman) and unsure of everything. I was just growing up is all it was. One thing I did know I was glad I met Jesus at 15 years old and I learned He will

Chapter One:

Where it all began

never fail me and if I just believe and put my Trust in Him and not people or money, He will be everything I'm not.

June 2000 I remember finally signing up for beauty school on North Texas Street in Fairfield California! I was so excited! When I found out Cosmetology covers hair care as well as skincare (Esthetics) and nail care (Manicurist/ Nail Tech) and once licensed I could be a manicurist or Esthetician or all three all I could picture in my mind was how much money I could make and how I could implement all three aspects of the beauty industry into my career!

No one told me Beauty School is tough! I had to learn chemistry and anatomy and physiology. No one told me upon signing up for my $20,000 education (all funded by the state because I was in high school and went through a certain program) that there is a science to mixing hair color and skincare products etc. Dear God I thought my head was going to explode from all of the information and I used to really struggle with retaining information. I am not mathematical…that's what calculators are for right? Also I was not prepared for the physical labor it takes to stand on your feet ALL DAY!

Furthermore, the girls…Not much home training, no filters, no manners, no etiquette and they did not worry about being polite at all. I thought about quitting because it was like I couldn't make a move without someone's nosy opinion, being a smarty-pants when all I wanted was my privacy to learn at my own pace. For being in school sixteen hundred hours you think I could have my learning style accommodated but oh no!

**Wisdom key #1: Do your research on your beauty/barber school!!**

If there is a school you want to attend, go there and get a service done in the area you want to specialize in and see how it goes. Interview the student that works on you and see what they say about the school.

**DON'T TELL THE STUDENT WORKING ON YOU RIGHT OFF THE BACK that you're interested in that particular school…just go to listen! THEY WILL TELL YOU THE TRUTH NINE TIMES OUT OF TEN!**

Beauty schools are unfortunately not what they were when I was in school and from being an instructor for eight years I can tell you the standard of instructors is not high either!

Most instructors are burnt out hairstylists that have to make a living and lack the passion you need to start a wonderful career. The reason many instructors lack passion is because they reflect ownership!

Chapter One:

Where it all began

15 years ago when I got my education I was afraid to disrespect the experience of my instructor, this entitled generation has no boundaries and the people who own the schools will let the students do whatever they want to keep the millions flowing through the schools. Beauty and barber schools have lost their structure that this generation needs and is lost without. I have sympathy for those students that are in the schools for the right reason which is to really learn!

Any instructor reading these words please don't compromise your quality for the few that are entrusted to you and won't listen to you because some do!

Don't stop pouring out your best while you're on the floor and there needs to be more of you to help every student. Please brush off the bad attitudes, the rebellions and defiance because your students that will carry on your techniques need you!

If you're looking to be a beauty/barber student make sure you have a plan while you're in school to focus on the science of what you're doing because you will face those same challenges at State Board which brings me to Wisdom Key #2:

**Wisdom Key #2: Never stop asking questions!**

If you're receiving federal funding AS SOON AS YOU SIGN ON THE DOTTED LINE YOU ARE EXPECTED TO FINISH WHAT YOU STARTED OR ANY MONEY PAID BY THE GOVERNMENT FOR YOUR EDUCATION WILL HAVE TO BE PAID BACK!

That's right! No free money! Unless the word GRANT is involved (which you will pay back over time in taxes) you better have a plan in place if you find out Barbering or Cosmetology or whatever program is not what you really want! ASK QUESTIONS!

Are you entitled to a refund if you're not happy with how things are going? When do you get your kit (the supplies you need to get through school)? What is in the kit? Are your tools quality or will they break on you in a month and should you put together your essentials that you'll need because you can be sure of the quality if you get what you need on your own? How long will it take for me to make money once in the field? What is the State Board passing rate? What are the school rules? May I have a copy of the curriculum? What will my day as a student here look like? What is involved in your disciplinary actions?

Chapter One:

Where it all began

If more schools were upfront with EVERYTHING they expect instead of making things up as time goes by there would be an abundance of schools training future professionals!

I can't tell you the number of schools I've worked in that were absolute pigsty's! Their run down, equipment falling apart, health hazards with the bare minimal to keep it running- look, if you have to beg a school owner to put some tuition money back into their investment that is not a place you need to be!

Make sure you ask that there is central heat and air conditioning! There is nothing like dryers and body heat to make you miserable during summer months and nothing like slow business time during rainy season and you need to be warm…ask the questions!

## Chapter 2

### Freshman room

**1 Peter 4:12- Dear friends don't be surprised at the fiery trials you are going through, as if some strange thing were happening to you**

I will never forget being stuck in a room with 24 other girls! Their conversations were inappropriate, I tried to stay to myself and then I was perceived as stuck up but I was really just very shy. I wanted the other girls to like me and be friends but my lack of skill had me so intimidated I didn't think anyone would like me.

By the time we were doing hair I couldn't even hold a comb correctly. I was constantly stressed and often I would run to the bathroom and cry during our breaks because I just didn't get it! I really wanted to do hair, it feels natural, it's glamourous but I wasn't getting it! It was like I was learning how to use the same hands I've had all my life!

On base, off base, half off base? What do I do before I start a chemical service to protect my client? There is so much to remember…take it slow. Stop thinking about what will happen if you mess it up…that's what you're supposed to do. That's how you learn. If you burn the hair it can be cut (if your instructor is doing what they're supposed too it won't get that far). If you cut too much it will grow back…have fun! So what if you're not as experienced as the student next to you, they're a student just like you are, there's no room to judge. Now don't make a mistake on a client because you're in school, I'm not saying to go around and purposely mess up people because you reap what you sow but allow yourself to make mistakes so you can grow. That's what had to happen to me for me to grow and by the end of this book you'll have an idea of how I came to be extremely successful in what I do and how what I did can work for you!

### Wisdom Key #3: Make sure your learning style is accommodated

Are you a hands on learner? A kinesthetic learner? Or audible learner meaning you learn more by listening and can do so while doodling on a piece of paper for example? The school you choose should be able to accommodate whatever your style of learning is.

Chapter Two:

Freshman Room

**Wisdom Key #4: Every school should have a no bullying policy!**

While we were learning how to cut hair that was the first time we had to build our cosmetologist muscles and stand during the whole thing! Our first 6 hours on our feet! By hour two I couldn't take it anymore and needed a chair. A forty or so year old woman yelled "La'Sandra, get up!" she said with a smirk. "I replied "why do I owe anyone an explanation for anything I do, if I sit down that's my business!" Why next did all 24 girls in the room start cussing me out? Of course the instructor was nowhere to be found and had nothing to say when she returned and wondered why there was so much tension in the air. I was seventeen years old and too young to realize because I was so quiet, the girls were just trying anything to provoke me to get a reaction and test my limits. They did that with each other, they did that with the instructors…no boundaries. I have never been so abused by strangers that knew nothing about me to judge me so harshly because they felt they could.

I went to the bathroom to clean my face and was reminded of my own issues. Please keep in mind every person you're in school with is coming with their own issues and does not deserve to be judged or condemned because life happens.

I was raised by my single father. My mother was too emotionally young to have children so my father raised me. I never connected with my mother during my adolescence and I didn't know how to connect with other women because the first one I ever met couldn't connect with me.

Maybe I was unworthy, unlovable and life would always be this way? I had feelings of not wanting to really live anymore. I wasn't good at anything, no one liked me…lies, lies, lies! Looking back I would have told myself "girl, get it together; this is only the beginning and the best is yet to come! Be encouraged!"

This is why you should practice not bringing your issues with you to school because you're putting yourself in a vulnerable situation for people to take advantage of your vulnerabilities. Life happens and you have to deal with it as it comes.

As time went on I joined another church that had the best praise and worship in Vallejo! I got really saved…I wasn't just a church goer anymore, I knew I had relationship with Jesus Christ, I read my bible every day and I still do and He was now with me in Beauty School! I received His love! The more I received, the more I gave. Jesus made me want to be good to everyone because He's been so good to me! God restored my mother and I and now we're best friends and you know what? Every girl in that school that I began with that put her mouth on me ended up dropping out, getting pregnant or quitting school for one reason or another. If you let God fight your battles and rest in Him, He will take care of you! (2 Chr. 20:15)

I forgave the girls that meant to hurt me. I learned to love my enemies and be good to them that used me for a verbal pin cushion!

Chapter Two:

Freshman Room

So it happened…I had a breakthrough when we were all learning how to do perms. Another student helped me! Just by pulling on the end papers to my perm I could roll the concave rod, untwist the band and snap the rod in place perfectly! Then on base, off base and half of base came naturally to me…and cutting? Please I didn't cut myself flying through haircuts until my fifth year in the business! I wasn't perfect but I was getting better!

**Wisdom Key #5: Keep telling yourself 'Every time I do this, I'm getting better at it!"**

Every haircut you do, every shave, every full set of nails, every wax you do is making you better! When I started barbering, using my razor around the hair line really tripped me up around the temple area and after 15 years that is my favorite place to shave!

As you embark on your new career please keep an open mind that it's your responsibility to be a leader! Just because there may be people around you that are lazy doesn't mean you have to do what everyone else is doing. Your career is a direct reflection of you and you will get out of it what you put into it and everything positive that you put into your career is making you better!

**Wisdom Key #6: Don't forget you're an individual!**

While you're in school you must keep yourself busy "WITHOUT THE USE OF YOUR CELL PHONE!" or whatever technology you carry around with you on a daily basis. In my salons cell phones are outlawed and if a stylist is on it on my floor I consider that unacceptable! No one wants to be in your chair while you're glued to your phone. You have the option to tell people to leave a message or you'll text them later. People that work for me cannot text on their phone and lounge in their stylist chair all day waiting for clients! I have a very high standard of cleanliness and right after I'm done with my clients I sanitize, sanitize, sanitize! No hair in my brushes, no color on the floor or on my clothes- no dirt and I expect the same from those who work with me!

Start good habits while you're in school and if you're assigned cleaning duties take advantage of them! You read right, CLEAN! Take time out to use blade wash on your clippers, disinfect your chair, trust me your clients appreciate it! If you take out time to read reviews online most reviews speak on cleanliness of the establishment. Would you eat in a dirty restaurant? No! People don't want to deal with dirt! Be an individual and a leader and your career will show its appreciation to you!

Also professionalism is contagious! If someone is being disrespectful to an instructor or a client, you can be an individual and decide not to join the crowd. That's right if your instructor has done nothing but help you, why give them an attitude because your friend doesn't like them? Being in beauty school turned me into an adult and adults leave school yard behavior back in elementary!

As I went out to the floor by myself I didn't realize there were a lot of habits and an etiquette I needed to incorporate my first experience in a salon environment which I will speak on in the next chapter.

I was so nervous because my class went from 24 down to 1…me. Now I had 300 pairs of eyes watching me and what kind of work I did and even more opinions. I loved my client's but I never got to do enough of certain services like haircuts on men, perms, weaves- the money making services. Some of my diva colleagues were too good to do pedicures because they didn't like feet so they were given to me and to this day I love clipping ingrown toenails and facials; who doesn't love popping a good zit? What about the satisfaction of extractions? Love them right? What services do you love? Strengthen them so you can broaden your horizons!

**Wisdom Key #8: Broaden your horizons and do what you're afraid of!**

How do you feel about ethnic textured hair? How about cutting straight hair? How about wig manufacturing and design? Have you thought about your brand? What do you specialize in? Build and focus on your strengths and then move on to what you're afraid of. Remember you're in this business to make money and support yourself, you can't do that just by eye brow waxing. If you can wax eye brows, you need to know how to thread them, wax them, draw them on, shave to shape them and everything that is in demand because if you're good at it, it should be making you rich!

## Chapter 3:

## Building your business before you leave school

**Zechariah 4:10- Do not despise small beginnings for the Lord loves to see the work begin (NLT emphasis mine).**

Most schools have a confidentiality clause meaning you cannot collect people's personal information. A school is not supposed to share your schedule with anyone, but if you receive a phone call they should take a message for you. You can have business cards made and hand them to the client though. Building your business when in school eases the pressure of building clientele once you leave. There are many companies you can find that will make you hundreds of professional looking business cards for pennies on the dollar! You are not jumping the gun, it is not too soon for you to have business cards and advertise! When you get your coffee, hand the barista your card. Going to the carwash? The people waxing your car have hair and skin and need your card. Getting groceries? The people checking you out at the counter need your services. Don't be afraid to build your business because you're in school, build your business because one day you're going to get out of school.

## Wisdom Key #9: Don't spend your tips!

What? You heard me right, it's never too early to start good habits with your money. You'd be amazed how much a dollar here and there can add up quickly which means unfortunately until you build up your nest egg of how ever much you're trying to achieve upon leaving school, NO EATING OUT! Having money for gas and your phone bill is one thing but eating out every day will cause you to rob yourself.

In the salon I still bring my lunch from home. One reason being I have had food poisoning from different places five times in my life. Also I sat down and added up one week I spent $102 eating out three times! That's gas, bridge toll and a utility that I ate! That $100 could have gotten me a little more ahead because in this life you never know what will happen or when you may pop a tire or have an unexpected expense and for beauty professionals things do come up.

Chapter three:

Building your business before you leave school

While in school I opened a bank account and would take my $20 a week and save it. While I was in school I paid cash for my supplies, products and equipment. When I graduated I paid cash to take my state board test. You see where I'm going?

Had I known then what I know now, my career would have been much different.

## Wisdom Key #10: Take advantage of extra training, seminars and shows locally and at your school

Is someone credible certifying you for extensions and fades etc.? Take advantage of that opportunity! The more paper you have the more $ paper you earn!

Also a good habit is the practice of not turning anyone away. Just because you've done three wet sets and a manicure and still have a few hours until you leave school doesn't give you the right to hang out in the parking lot, lunch room or where ever to avoid taking more people because you don't want to be used as labor for the school. To tell you the truth ALL CLIENTS ARE practice! Your school may make $1000 a day from services which is barely enough to keep the lights on!

Don't start out your professional reputation as someone that's inconsistent and unreliable. In the salon world, I don't know what a break or a lunch is. I eat standing up! I don't stop usually but to stuff some fruit or nuts in my mouth (I call my snacks pop-a-ble's because it's something I can easily pop in my mouth and keep going). Time is money and the more time I stop, the less I'm making!

Long story short make sure you do whatever you can to ensure you have a long lasting business. Don't go through all the training and discipline not to use it- you're too good for that and the rewards are great!

## Wisdom Key#11: Don't worry about what is none of your business!

Simple. If someone is having a conversation that has nothing to do with you or what you're doing it's best not to get involved. For example, if you "overheard" that your work at school is modern day slavery (because they do get busy at times) you can demonstrate leadership

Chapter three:

Building your business before you leave school

and stick to what you know. It's not your business what your school is doing with your tuition money or whoever you work for, how much money they make off what you do. If you think a situation is unfair then leave!

In every school I've worked for, behind the scenes they were struggling. No matter their tuition rate. Why? I'm from California and stuff is expensive! A studio apartment in San Francisco goes for $6,000 A MONTH! – it costs more to live here than in New York! Not to mention water, electricity, internet, taxes, paying back loans taken out to get the school open, living expenses, you name it, it's expensive! If you think about it, it is slowly becoming impossible for people to live on their own!

Assumption concerning anything you don't know and jumping to conclusions is not going to help you in any area of your life. When it comes down to it, take care of and be concerned about you. Not what other people are doing; take care of you!

As we continue on in this book I am going to show you red flags of employment and everything else I know about not getting taken advantage of in the work place. However nine times out of ten, minding your own business saves you a lot of headaches.

Chapter three:

Building your business before you leave school

# Chapter 4

## Customer service

**1 Peter 4:10- As each has received a gift, use it to serve one another, as good stewards of God's varied Grace.**

I love barbers but I cannot stand going to the barbershop! I travel frequently so that situation forces me to try barbershops that I have never been in before. The average barbershop has left me standing in the front looking dumb for more than ten minutes at a time! For ten minutes I'm standing there waiting to be acknowledged. Someone say "hi" to me! Someone ask me what I need! Someone help me!

Those that know me know I get an undercut and sideburn angled touch up with a hard line. An undercut is the hair in my nape area up to below my occipital bone line is tapered into a number 1 guard, (from being bald to my skin up to 3 millimeters and my sideburns are cut at an angle because I like to think they are the mark the Bronx New York left on me and I wear them proudly!)

Don't assume because I'm a girl I'm standing there looking for a date! Try not to let more than ten seconds go by without acknowledging people that come through your door.

Your level of customer service will make or break your business!

There are some students I could not tell were fresh out of school and have such wonderful customer service you would think they were born into the business! You must have such an understanding of customer service entering into the field because without it you can single-handedly kill your business!

## Wisdom Key #11: You never know who is in your chair! Be careful how you treat everyone!

There was a time I was working in a salon and an average looking man in a white shirt and blue jeans bought $200 worth of products and a few in travel sizes. I won't go into detail but I knew exactly who this man was but no one else seemed to know. This man is a movie director and is native to Marin County in California…wow. I am not a start struck person but I love a man that is family oriented and creative and has touched generations with his work and I hope to do the same. Also, he was like any other customer I've served; very down to earth and nice. Imagine if he sent his children to receive services from me or if he sent his wife? Referrals are the most important aspect of your clientele. How will people know about you if they haven't heard about you? Give all of your clients something to talk about! Serve them water, ask if they'd like a magazine, give them a deep conditioner or let them try some of your products in their hair. In this day and age you must go above and beyond because people can go anywhere.

People can go to their cousin, or friend that does hair in their garage but they come to you. Make their experience worth it when people come to you!

## Wisdom Key #12: The people you work with and work for are your customers like anyone else!

Yes your colleagues, coworkers, instructors, everyone around you is a relationship you need. This doesn't mean you have to be in love with everyone just for the heck of it. This principle and wisdom key implies the fact you must remain mindful as a professional to work well with those around you. You must learn to accommodate every personality type because whether you realize it or not YOU ARE BEING WATCHED!

Why are you being watched? Because excellence is something people admire. People need something and someone to look up to and who holds the standard? YOU! Make it a habit while you are in school to not just be nice but practice customer service. How do you want to be treated? Do that!

### Provide customer service to those around you!

It only takes two minutes to wipe out a shampoo bowl with a clean towel after you used it for the next person to bring their client to. It helps when you see your coworker finish with a haircut and you sweep their hair up for them to help them move their customers along. People appreciate you not leaving a mess for everyone else to clean up at the end of the day when everyone is trying to go home…THINK OF OTHER PEOPLE!

Why? The way you conduct yourself at work says everything people need to know about your character! If you work messy and always have a cluttered workspace that gives people the perception of a messy minded person. I'm not trying to be offensive, I'm giving you a sense of reality through my writing and experience. There's only so many times I'm going to keep telling the same person to clean up after themselves before I decide it's best that we part ways…I'm just saying. After I've invested my life and money into my businesses the last thing I will tolerate is grown people that don't clean up after themselves. When you occupy another persons' business space that is what we're thinking most of the time. The majority of state board fines comes from uncleanliness and whose responsibility are those? The person whose license is displayed!

Chapter Four:

Customer Service

## YOUR LEVEL OF CUSTOMER SERVICE IS HOW YOU TEACH OTHER PEOPLE HOW TO VALUE YOU!

### Wisdom Key #13: What is a filter and how do I decide what is acceptable in my work environment and what is not? Think about it!

To tell the truth most clients want to talk about themselves and what's going on with their hair, not about you and what your boyfriend and girls were up to last night! You're not friends with every client, they are paying you money to be heard and have their needs met and come back for their next appointment!

SOME THINGS MUST STAY PRIVATE!

Where you live, how much money you make, your phone conversations- NO ONE NEEDS TO KNOW THAT! What a filter plainly is; its purpose is that brief moment that you think to yourself, "should I say this or not?" "Will this offend someone?" "Is this something I would say in front of my kids or parents?" "Should this be public information?

It is offensive and appalling for people to disrespectfully talk about other professionals! Barbers on average don't do that because they have an unspoken brotherhood between men and are more comfortable around each other. Women on the other hand can be more verbally destructive to each other!

### Wisdom Key #14: Those that gossip to you gossip about you!

And you can take that to the bank!

It is unprofessional:

o       No one really wants to hear about your sex life, sexual preferences (as far as positions), how drunk or high you got or get- it is unprofessional!

o       Your textbook should also make you aware that it's unprofessional to talk about religion, sexual orientation, politics or protected groups. THERE IS MORE TO LIFE! Talk about the weather, what's the last book you read, a movie you saw-did you like it? Why? Don't find yourself in the middle of a lawsuit for a difference of opinions. Watch what you talk about you will save yourself a lot of trouble!

Chapter Four:

Customer Service

o      It is unprofessional to keep a blunt rolled behind your ear during working hours and while you're working on someone. You may think "they don't care as long as their hair looks good" but what are you advertising? What image are you projecting? Are you average or are you exceptional?

o      To come to work and do your hair, make up, nails, shave etc. You must come to work prepared with your makeup and hair already done! Why? When I pay my money I expect to receive what you project. If you're a makeup artist what are you doing barefaced at work? Where's the drama as far as makeup goes? As far as your makeup style; make it pop, show me on your face how you can make my skin look like butter when it looks like cottage cheese, come on and transform me! You are how you show me what you can do!

o      To be late! I hate! Things come up and there are emergences that you can call and inform who you need to about certain things. One thing that gets under my fingernail is if you have clients waiting on you to arrive at work for more than ten minutes is unprofessional and grounds for termination in most work facilities. If you live fifteen minutes from work you need to leave thirty-five minutes early for work. Set up when you come in, "don't get ready, be ready" and people do notice and appreciate you making the effort to be prepared and taken for their appointments!

## Wisdom key #15: Avoid the phrase "I don't know."

It is very aggravating when someone has questions, they need answers and if you don't know the answers it's your responsibility to find who does! That is being efficient and the most that people can ask of you if you don't know an answer to a question. Don't give out bad and incorrect information, find the right answers from a source who knows definitely!

## Wisdom key #16: Don't be afraid to ask for help!

Again someone has the answer you need! Nine times out of ten you work around someone you can bring your questions too and if not why are you there if no one is interested in seeing you grow? Don't take a chance and jump into a color correction of someone who colored their hair black and now want to be platinum blonde! It ain't gonna happen! Not in one setting. It is going to take a lot of money and time to strip the black color and start all over without frying the hair! Also if the client used black "dye" from a box and that dye is metallic, I wouldn't chance taking the opportunity for growth on without a waiver being signed to protect myself!

Good customer service involves being willing to help out your coworkers. If a new nail tech is having a hard time with smile lines for a French manicure; someone has to be willing to show them how to choose which brush or tool to help them create a great French tip!

I am going to revisit the subject of customer service throughout this book and hopefully offer good advice to anyone who wants to own their own business some day!

Chapter Four:

Customer Service

# Chapter 5

## Okay I'm done with school now what?

**2 Timothy 2:15- Study to show yourself approved unto God, a workman who need not be ashamed, rightly dividing the word of truth.**

Had I known then what I know now…before I graduated I would have been looking for a place to work. If only I could do hair really well. If only I knew where to go. I didn't know what I wanted from a work place. I didn't know where to begin.

It didn't occur to me that my school felt their job stopped at getting me to state board. I wasn't ready for the salon. I had no business sense what so ever. Honestly between you and I , the first five years of my career, every place I worked at bent me over a barrel financially and I will get into that later in the chapter. Social media was not what it was back then for me to network and I had no idea what was in store for me, I was a seventeen year old girl that had never been on the internet... I didn't know how to use it!

Back then I had to have a live model for the state board test and she flaked on me! I found a random girl in the parking lot in Fairfield California and I didn't pass my test because she had acrylic nails and I couldn't do the sculptured nail on her or any nail services. The second time I got turned away at the door because my name was different on my driver's license then it was on my admission letter! The third time, my mother was my model and I passed!

I was an officially licensed Cosmetologist that still couldn't do hair! I couldn't cut, color was a mystery to me and cut men's hair? Forget about it! I didn't realize it until years later that I failed myself back in Beauty School because I thought I knew everything and I knew nothing! My school failed me in the sense that they only made sure I knew enough to pass the State Board, they didn't care if I made it in the salon so I could have a life! This whole time it was just about money? Really? All the customer service, etiquette and professionalism I learned in the field and it should be a schools responsibility to educate the student for their career. Passing a test is easy, building a career is a beast.

**Wisdom Key #17: Know where you're going before you get there!**

I have some suggestions for you before you leave school:

Chapter Five:

I'm done with school now what?

While you're in school know your culture before you leave! Not your skin color; your culture! If you're a punk rocker, don't work in a suit and tie environment! You don't fit in that culture! If you're a colorist, don't work in a location that primarily cuts hair; you'll be miserable because you can't create like you want too!

What is a culture? Your way of doing things is a culture. For example hip hop is a culture. The way a hip hop fan has ideas of fashion, the way a hip hop artist talks and uses their lingo is a culture. As a beauty professional your culture may be color and how you execute it. As a barber the way you execute your chairside manner and handle customer service is your culture. You decide how you want to get through life that is your culture.

You must have a goal, you must fulfil your purpose and commit to it because where you decide to work is much like being in a marriage. Your career cannot be a good one without your commitment.

While in school find out what works for you. Can you deal with having a part-time job to support yourself while building your clientele? Odds are when you first graduate you are not going to see a return on your investment (that you spent on school) for your first 6 months to a year! Yes it's true YOU ARE NOT GOING TO TURN INTO A ROCKSTAR OVER NIGHT JUST BECAUSE YOU HAVE YOUR LICENSE!

My first salon job involved this woman I idolized. She owned a very successful salon in Vallejo and I watched her do some hair! She made her money! $65 quick weaves, $150 colors and all before 2p.m on an average day and everyone working for her in the salon paid booth rent…could you imagine? She promised me before I got licensed that when I did I could have a chair in her shop. In my next chapter I'm going to explain how not to get played or pimped in the business but let me explain my career foundation first.

She let me work in her salon to wash hair which was illegal but I didn't know that, all I knew is I wanted to be like her. Her sons wore gold jewelry, she paid cash for her cars and owned a house. She was a fast talker and started me off as an assistant. I shampooed hair and swept floors. I'm proud of that. I was the one running to get everyone's lunch and doing beauty supply runs…she would tip me money here and there. Let me make it clear I was not an employee on payroll- I was cheap labor which was also illegal but again I didn't know. I was with her for six months before I had the nerve to ask "what about the chair you promised me?" She also said I could do walk-ins (people that came in with no appointment) which she passed to the other girls working for her…it wasn't fair. Finally one day I came in and took my tools and left.

One day I was walking around a mall and I saw a salon that looked nice and people that were my age worked in it. I was eighteen by this time and just started community college because I still didn't know what I wanted to do. Cosmetology was my fall back plan incase anything else I did didn't work out. I got hired and then a new manager came who was also my same age. The environment was a corporate owned salon chain, one of the biggest salon chains

Chapter Five:

I'm done with school now what?

in the world and they had a lot of rules. I couldn't come and go as I pleased. There was a dress code of all black. I was told when to go to lunch and when to go home, when to sit and there was retail involved. I like selling retail, I didn't like selling retail to make someone else rich though. I sold thousands of dollars for my paycheck to look like something I keep in my cookie jar now. Spare change. I didn't know God was using that situation to teach me how to develop and sell my own products though. I just didn't see it. I didn't know it was a law to take breaks every four hours…I found out when I got fired for it! Two months later. I was starting to build clientele and I had no one's information for them to follow me so…back to square one.

I started in another salon in Vallejo and the owner just wanted $100 a week. I thought to myself "I can do that!" I WAS BROKE! For months my bank account was in the red! I was constantly coming out of pocket because I thought someone was going to be there to hand me clients like the last place I worked. Oh no! I learned no one in this life is going to hand you or me anything because I feel like you and I deserve it! Wow. I sat day in and day out waiting for people. Bored out of my mind. No one taught me how to go out and hustle, pass out business cards or anything to help myself. Guess what? THERE WERE 0 WALK-INS.

Eventually people from my church that was across the street helped me out every now and again but I wanted my business to be like the first lady I mentioned. Something I didn't notice at the time was my skill was getting sharper and better. At the time I used to go to my car and cry because I didn't know where to go or what to do. This dream I had was not paying off very well. I wanted to go shopping and walk into a store and buy a designer hand bag because I could, I didn't want to pay my dues. I didn't want to hurt. I would pray and ask God "is this what you want me to do? My coworkers laugh at me and the owner I'm afraid she wouldn't want me there because I'm not able to do much." I was so scared things would always be that way. The owner and I had our differences because I wanted to be in an upscale salon, not some run down hole in a wall! Why was I there? That wasn't my culture! I am bi-racial and I work in American environments with intellectual edgy people that drink coffee and read the newspaper. I was born in San Jose and raised in Oakland (Piedmont is an old Jewish community in North Oakland to be specific). Oakland is my kind of diverse people but I am not "hood". That's my culture. My culture is also centrally heated and air conditioned but anyway my point is I settled way below my potential because I compared myself to someone that is not of my same culture. What happened next? I continued to bump my head over and over and over again until I decided to do something different…succeed no matter what!

So before I knew it eight years passed by and by then I had worked in corporate owned salons and independently owned salons and one thing I found was that they were pretty much all the same. They were the same in the sense that I either provided everything or the more someone contributed to my business (providing products, overhead, lighting, towels etc) the less I made. The more I provided for myself, the more I got to keep! In 2008 I thought I was done! I was going to retire from doing hair, selling other people's retail and go back to working for corporate as a district manager. I was after a consistent income which I thought this company would provide. I ended up working at managing over ten

Chapter Five:

I'm done with school now what?

stores from Sacramento to Monterey California. I worked sometimes over 50 hours a week and it didn't matter because I was paid by salary…retail wage. What ended up happening was total sabotage, I didn't realize when you have a job that holds a little bit of power that other people lust after an covet that job as well. There were three people working under me that were waiting for me to slip up to get my job and what they did worked. I was out of work again because I trusted a company that I thought would protect me against what other people said. I got my hair done on the clock. Which I did not, the store was closed and the stylist was clocked out as well, I was never on any clock. One of the stores I was over still had holiday sigs up in January and one of the locations had a girl who could not cut men's hair and they sat a man in her chair anyway. I saw her struggling so I cut the man's hair…I got fired for those things. Stupid and nothing was a company violation. Someone else wanted my job is all and I did not think anyone would stoop so low for my little $900 bi-weekly job. The thirst is real! Also I knew I was fired unlawfully but the company I worked for knew I wouldn't fight because who could be able to afford an attorney on my wages and defend me for something I could not prove?

## Wisdom Key #18: Educate yourself on your work rights!

If you work for a corporate salon do you know when you're entitled to have your breaks? Do you have a system of keeping track of your own hours? Do you have to fight to get your paychecks? What if they need correcting do you know who you talk to about that?

The next chapter in this book may be the most important subject I have ever written about in my entire career. I am going to break down what to look out for when finding a place to work and teach you how to develop your kind of culture that works for you. Also I will show you the difference between someone that is interested in helping you grow as a professional and who is just looking to pimp your gifts.

## Chapter 6

## How not to get pimped!

**James 1:5- If any of you lacks wisdom, let him ask God who gives generously to all without reproach, and it will be given him.**

As you can see I have been through a ringer in my career! My goal with my career now is to help as many people as I can to avoid the things I went through.

What does it mean to get pimped? A prostitute gets paid to be taken advantage of right? A job can be the same position just a different circumstance. How do you avoid getting paid to be taken advantage of?

I'm sorry but if you're doing $200 of work a day and your paycheck matches your shoe size, I'm sorry, you're getting paid to be taken advantage of! If you're putting out way more than you're being given, you're being taken advantage of!

Early on in my career I lacked the wisdom it took to make my career successful. I didn't have common sense to do the math of the work that I was doing and comparing to what I took home.

I FELL FOR IT! Over and over again I believed what people told me instead of waiting on the proof and then I realized I was caught up in a bad situation. I believed whatever a shop owner told me "I guarantee you a $750 paycheck" or "You will be making $30-$45 an hour!" I fell for it! They didn't have anything to prove to me what they were saying I was so naïve I figured they wouldn't lie to me. It never occurred to me that some people just needed a warm body in a position to make them their money.

**Wisdom Key #19: Anyone promising you a set dollar amount to come and work for them is probably lying!**

I am sorry to inform you that people lie! YOU ARE IN A SHARK TANK WHETHER YOU REALIZE IT OR NOT! Anyone promising you $5,000 a month is purely (forgive me for being crass) blowing smoke up your caboose! This is the person that see's so much potential to make money off what you could bring into their business that YOU FAIL TO REALIZE THEY NEED you more than you need them!

•       Who can give you a testimonial to making a person that was an employee into a rock star? People you work for are trying to retire from the work you do THE MAJORITY OF OWNERS IS NOT IN THIS BUISINESS TO HELP THOSE "BEANEATH" THEM RETIRE BEFORE THEY DO!"

•       People in our business are given three options:

1.      Work for hourly wage

2.      Work on commission

3.      Rent a space

Those of us working for an hourly wage are controlled more. You are told when to come in to work, when to leave etc. Yes you get paid for slow times you're sitting and there are no clients and you are in a great position to build clientele however, your income is controlled and limited. "But you get 10% of your retail sales" and "you get to keep your tips." Yes but you're still living at home with $400 to get you through the next two weeks. Is this your culture?

Working on commission: means you may have set times you work but you make a certain percentage of what you do. For example, many commission rates top out at 50% which means the services you do for $10, you get $5. Therefor your high ticket items are where you will receive a significant increase. However you are entirely responsible for your own taxes! If you don't pay taxes the IRS will find you! Please save yourself a head ache and keep track of your tips, services and clients you'll thank me for it if you get audited!

When you rent a space: you pay a set amount of rent once a month and depending where you live that could be any amount. You provide everything yourself, your tools, products, marketing collateral and everything.

Chapter 6:

How not to get pimped

I know people in Oakland that pay $1000 a month and live very well with living expenses and all. For some people that is their culture. You have to come in to this business knowing what you want and what your limits are. For me my kryptonite is children...the moving is what is hard for me to deal with. We get through it and I've never messed up a little kid but if I can pass that service to my co-worker I will!

**Can you get fired from a commission or rent situation?**

Absolutely! Whoever owns your establishment has the right to tell you where to go! When you own a salon or barbershop- meaning you are on the lease then no one can tell you anything! You have arrived at the top of the service providing chain! Between you and I, the people that own are the ones that stay around longest in this business. Even when you're an owner, you must beware!

I do not sign yearlong leases. Its 6 months or nothing. Why? I don't know if I like the landlord. If I don't own the building and the roof leaks, whose responsibility is that? What's in your lease is what you have to live with and are bound to until the lease is up. If I don't have a good relationship with the landlord and they don't fix things or uphold their part of our agreement 6 months is not a long time to deal with that and it's a little easier to move my business! Just some fruit for thought. People that I do business with, we have known each other for years and I shopped and did my homework and we fit in each other's culture.

Likewise if your landlord doesn't like you, or what you're doing they do have the right not to lease to you again.

**Wisdom Key #20- Get everything you need in writing no matter what!**

It doesn't matter if who you're working with is someone you've known all of your life. To make sure you have everything you have been promised, you need to demand to have everything in writing.

What you need to get in writing from anyone you work for:

Chapter 6:

How not to get pimped

1. What your wages are and how and when you're paid!

2. What time you're expected to work.

3. What is supplied and what do you supply as far as tools and products.

4. How are the clients and walk-in's rotated throughout the business? Is the rotation by who gets to the salon (or place of business) first in the beginning of the day or is it by who needs the most money?

5. Expectations and rules- what is expected of you and what do you expect from the place of work?

6. What is the incentive you will receive for working in the place of business you choose? In other words "what's in it for you?"

7. Are there benefits? What happens if you're playing ball and fall and break your wrists? What do you do?

8. What if you're starting from the bottom and have no clientele?   How long do you have to build before you're cut off?

I know it's hard to imagine that this business can be so cut throat but it can be. Hopefully I've provided some good advice for you to decide what you want and what is best for you.

As I mentioned before I've worked for every kind of salon and what was the most unfair scenario in my opinion is when I found a salon owner was giving my clients away to my coworker because she was a single mother and because I wasn't married with children I didn't need the money as much. Is that discrimination that can be proven in a court of law? It was betrayal at its best. Erasing my clients off the books and putting them on someone else's huh?

I had one better for her! I was living in Atlanta Georgia at the time and I packed my bags and moved to New York! I was tired of working with people I couldn't trust and at least in New York it is what it is! I moved to the Bronx and since I had just finished my instructor training in Georgia and working at the same time, I went to instruct in a school in the Bronx.

Why did a fight break out my first day there? The majority of the time I spent there I loved it! I loved the food, the people and the shopping but unfortunately I got home sick and I wasn't making enough money.

## Chapter 6:

### How not to get pimped

Eventually I got back home and became a salon manager for yet another corporate salon chain. I don't remember working so hard to keep that going and it didn't make enough money as a whole and it closed.

They sent me to another one of their salons promising me that things would be better this time and still I didn't have enough money and I left. I went to work for a child care center and was even broker plus those little children had malaria (I'm exaggerating!) There wasn't a month I worked there that I wasn't sick. I didn't want to do hair anymore! I'd had enough! I made up in my mind that hair wasn't what I thought it was and I was never going to do it again!

I later began working at a huge retail store (trust me you've shopped there) and I was a cosmetics counter manager for a cosmetic line no one has ever heard of. However I took to makeup naturally. I learned techniques from every major cosmetic line on the market and I was fortunate to go to a few of their trainings as well.

There was a random young lady who was a tomboy running around the store with her wedding dress in her arms and everyone at the salon downstairs was booked. I couldn't help it…I wanted to rescue her and I grabbed her and we went to the counter and I pulled her hair into an up do and the few hair products we were selling I used the sample bottles from the display and whipped her hair and did her makeup. She was so thankful and she caused me to remember the love I have for doing hair.

### Wisdom Key #21: Stay true to yourself!

Don't ever let people that don't walk in your shoes to dictate where they feel you should be or what you should be doing. Yes you should make plans; no you shouldn't be lazy about them!

I'm sure you're probably wondering "Why didn't you quit?" or "You could have done something else?" "Are you sure hair is what you're supposed to be doing?" I'll answer that for you!

No matter what walk of life you come from "You must walk out your own faith". No one could teach me the lessons that my journey has taught me in a classroom. Jesus never promised me a perfect life and I am not entitled to have everything come to me easily because I'm saved but I AM NEVER ALONE IN ANYTHING! How else could I move from State to State and "stumble" upon jobs?

Chapter 6:

How not to get pimped

Who else would give me the favor to have a corporate job with no prior experience? This was all in God's plan believe it or not. He wrote it all out because I had to get this all together to have something to write.

Nothing just happens, there are no coincidences or accidents. Again some things I suffered were because of mistakes I made and there are consequences but who gave me the grace to get through? As much disappointment and betrayal I've suffered, some people have commit suicide over those very same things. I totally understand being gifted and can't share it or having hope in something I do well but it doesn't seem like it's paying off. I understand.

What does this have to do with not getting pimped? You can't let what people, the media or what society says about life define your standards of what you want. That's also how you avoid getting pimped is by not letting people control your thoughts!

When it comes to my story, you haven't seen anything yet...stay tuned!

In the next chapter I will show you what it takes to make $100,000 in a year and how to achieve wealth. There is a difference between being successful and being wealthy.

## Chapter 7

## How to achieve wealth

**Deuteronomy 8:18- But remember the Lord your God. He is the one who gives you power to be successful (the ability to produce wealth), in order to fulfill the covenant he confirmed to your ancestors with an oath. (Emphasis mine)**

In the beginning of 2013 I was in a horrible car accident. I did three 360's which means I hydroplaned in a rain storm and hit the center divide on the highway. My car spun completely around three times and the last time I was flying backwards and facing traffic. I screamed "Jesus! Jesus! Jesus!" and Jesus showed up! I felt a warm blanket lay on me and hold me in my car. My back windshield busted all over the place and **not one** shard of glass ever hit me! The police showed up and gave me a ticket for "failure to stay in my lane" and that day I told my father "I want to move back to California."

No one was hurt. I wasn't hurt. Thank God! That was the worst $430 I ever wasted on a ticket! I didn't stay in Georgia long enough to fight it, I was gone less than two weeks later. I took it as a sign because things weren't getting any better. I moved there during the mass exodus in 2008 along with one million other people that moved to Atlanta. From then on I saw for myself how short life can be.

**Wisdom Key #22: Life is too short...make some decisions about what you want now...procrastination is a killer!**

As I touched down in SFO I almost kissed the asphalt when my feet touched home. Atlanta wasn't a bad place...just not the place for me. The pay rate does not match the cost of living and there is still a lot of ignorance there. I was there five years including the time I spent in New York. A few months later I began working at a Barber college as an instructor. I worked my way up working the night shift. I had never worked for men before...beautiful men! They're so easy going and they don't like drama! They cut hair in ways I had never seen as a cosmetologist. The college opened at the beginning of the Barber surge and now every month in the Bay Area it seems someone is having a barber battle (competition for barbers) somewhere. Female barbers are at a record high and the rate of barbershops opening in the Bay Area are at a record rate. At last I saw the consistency I longed for! In the beginning we had our ups and downs but six months into my time there, I saw the hot mess it really was...just like every other school. This school was brand new and the students paid out of pocket for the program and everything they didn't get they pouted over!

One time they didn't have a class sign up and that had never happened before so I started doing odd jobs around the school to keep a job. I was the receptionist, administrator, janitor and maid (cleaning bathrooms and sweeping and mopping floors qualifies anyone as a janitor and maid). I did those things with pleasure because as a single father I remember helping my father as a child when he was a janitor. I remember my mother being an administrator for a children's hospital so I did those things with pride. I even made it fun for myself.

The students...no matter where I worked I love to watch them learn things from me. I love to teach and educate! So you know the truth yes "Teachers all have our favorites!" However that didn't affect the grades of my students and I came to school every day laughing because my students brought me so much joy!

### Wisdom Key #23: Wealth is in your fun!

If you're not doing what makes you happy you're going to be miserable! That's the first stage of attaining wealth- not money! Real wealth is building on your strength as I said before.

### Wealth brings you money that won't run out!

Unfortunately reality hit and I was determined to make my homecoming a rewarding one! No one knew at the time except when I started working for my barber college's direct competition! Only thirty minutes apart too! One paid me more and I worked in the morning and the other I worked in the evening and my schedule never conflicted. The competing barber college had two locations so I worked two jobs in three locations and I had never made so much money in my life! I got sick as a dog working 60 hours a week! One day the competing college owner called me and let me go...no reason, no real explanation...nothing.

I had another job to fall back on so they knew I wasn't butt out or anything. As I mentioned before the original Barber college I worked for was a hot mess behind closed doors. There was so much greed and favoritism and there were two owners and one liked hiring his family and friends to work there! I didn't mind the family but the friends were unreliable and unethical. Also my direct supervisor was a sneaky woman. She sabotaged everything I did and all behind my back while smiling in my face. If I had an idea, she made it her own. If I made a suggestion she would okay it and then change it to fit what she wanted to do. The owners loved and practically worshiped her and I have no idea why. Furthermore I "felt" she didn't like me and I had no idea why. I asked her constantly if I was doing okay and meeting her expectations and she would say "yes". When I saw the games she would play of course I had no real loyalty to that company. Loyalty was too much to ask of me. Every other month they would change my schedule from working 3-5 days a week to working the same amount of days only 4 hours a day and this went on almost two years.

A small group of the students didn't think I had the right to teach there because I wasn't a barber. I was hired as a cosmetologist and before it came down to it I realized I wasn't getting anywhere and I better make the best of a bad situation. I love the creative barber culture and it was becoming my passion. I love to shave. I love to cut and I love my male clientele! I never imagined I would ever be a licensed barber. My teachers were my students. Some of them got aggravated when I would watch because I was their instructor and they felt I was stalking them and they would report me to the owners but they didn't know how this craft drew me in! I was watching because that's my learning style and how I learn.

At that time another beauty college needed help and hired me within the week! Who can explain when one door closes God will create a new one!

Oh my goodness I was worked more than ever! On top of that my coworker at the beauty school owned a shop and took me on for Mondays only at her salon up the street. I worked with senior citizens and I loved it! I love talking with all of the people with wealth and wisdom and they taught me some things I will share with you now!

### Wisdom Key #24: Write the vison and make it plain

I've said it before and I'll say it again if you don't write down what to focus on you can't attain it because your mind will change a million different times before it focuses on one thing.

### Wisdom Key #25: The secret of the world's wealthiest people is:

### "Multiple streams of income"

That's right I mentioned having businesses as well as books, bath and body care line, a skin care line for men and much more. What could you do well at the same time while building in your profession? I've always wanted to own a manufacturing company. Does that have anything to do with hair? Possibly, I want to manufacture different bottles and be the source for people to come and get unusually shaped bottles for their products.

### $416.65

Remember that is the goal you should set for yourself every day.

$416.65x 5 Days a week= $2,083

$2,083 a week x 4 weeks is $8,332 a month

$8,332 a month is $100,000 a year!

Now how will you maintain $416.65 a day? That is your million dollar question. What are the services you provide that will cause you to bring home $416.65 after taxes? How about selling retail? Shirts, hats, purses, nail polish, make up, body oil? Have a customer appreciation event in the form of a fight party and charge people $20 to get through your door and get a hot dog or something! Get creative! As many times as I have been jobless, I know how to pull a monkey out of my hat to collect my coins for me, while other magicians are playing around with rabbits! Going to other people's houses to do services for them is not the safest line of work but if you know the client well enough; there are options.

If you break it down you can see the possibility. What would you do with $100,000? What if there is a day that you missed your goal? In the retail world anything you miss one day will get added on to the next and your best will never be good enough. I'm not suggesting that retail jobs aren't good because they are I'm saying no matter how much you make the company you work for, it will never be enough!

I always encouraged my students with the same principles I'm sharing with you. Live within your means while you plan on your dreams! You can do more and more as time goes on...millions aren't for everyone. I'm just laying out examples for you to give you some options you may want to consider.

## Wisdom Key #26: Be ready to give it time

There is no way around it, you must be patient! It takes time to build and do what you do. It takes time to see a return on any investment you make. Be patient while you attain your goal. No it's not easy; sometimes it hurts. It hurts when you sacrifice going out with your friends because you're focused on your purpose. It's hard going through financial difficulty and trying to achieve your purpose. It will pay off if you're consistent. You can't decide one day you don't feel like doing certain services just because. Doing feet and popping zits for people brings in money I mean someone has to do it! (I know that last sentence was gross but I added it to make you smile hopefully!)

## Just remember you have to make your goal!

It was during this time I started thinking about my own legacy and brand. There is a story in the bible in the book of Genesis about a man named Joseph. He was betrayed by his own brothers and sold into slavery. He was accused of a crime he didn't commit and was sent to prison for years. Then the king had a problem only Joseph could solve. By the power of God he met the kings need and was made the greatest man in the kingdom. How's that for a come up? Joseph maintained his integrity even though he had the right to be angry and plead his innocence. God did it for him. While Joseph was going through prison, he learned the language because unbeknownst to him, God was moving him to the palace!

I mentioned that because every place I've been whether in California in corporate or in Georgia in a school, I learned how to speak this industries' language. Why? I didn't know where God was taking me but looking back I saw how He was moving!

I saw the biggest needs in this industry and I intend to meet them with the best of my ability! I will cover more of this in the next chapter but for now I want you to consider your journey. Have cycles kept repeating themselves with the same result? Maybe that's because you keep missing the lesson?

Why is there always personality conflict? Why is the shop owner or manager always trying to get over on me? Why is it I don't last long at certain places? Have you ever thought maybe it's not about you? Maybe it's all about your learning experience that's making you better? Just a suggestion. If you're looking for what God is telling you about you through your situations, look at what you can't stand!

I'm sorry to give you a little tough love but I've worked with hundreds of people and students and here are some things I have found all Beauty and Barber, Nail Tech and Massage Therapists have in common and perhaps you can put some names in each category:

- **Every business has a snitch:** stay on your toes and watch them more than they watch you. A snitch is a nosy jealous person that will build on your weakness and are so weak themselves they report your behavior and every move to the boss hoping for recognition. They have nothing better to do. If they have nothing to report, they will find something. Remember WATCH!
- **Watch out for people that talk too much!** People that talk too much and brag about things usually lie. If you haven't seen the fly car and fine spouse...there's a possibility someone is making false claims. Also if someone is extremely quiet, that type is usually sneaky. I'm not talking about people that aren't big talkers I mean the one's that sit and watch and stare at everything. Never assume you're not being watched.
- **Your net worth does not determine your worth:** When speaking of assets and how much a person has is their "net worth". Please don't hate me for speaking freely but it's okay if you do. I do not listen to, buy or play hip hop music of any kind at home or at any of my businesses.  Most hip-hop glorifies money, clothes and loose women...stuff. We at my businesses listen to R&B or instrumental jazz, that is it. I don't support anything that is cussing us all out! I work too hard to allow that. For someone to degrade women with the B word disrespects me, my mother and every woman around. I do not like cussing, it's ugly and filthy and not ladylike. I do not encourage violence, resistance to the law or defiance at all. In fact I don't support any image that has had a negative effect on our society at large and I respectfully decline from things that are negative. You will never walk into A Beauty Bar™ and see a half-naked man or nudity at all in the artwork on my walls. I encourage the family to come together to get pampered and I don't want mothers shielding their children's eyes when they walk through my doors. **Image is everything**. I set an atmosphere that relaxes people when they walk through my doors. We make people feel comfortable. The barbers that work with me wear their pants on their hips and the Cosmo's working with me are not allowed to wear anything 2 ¾ inches below their collar bone.
- **Make sure you work in a place willing to invest in you as much as you are in them:** forget training and learning how to answer phones, what about continuing education? In this technological age where everything is available at the click of a button there should be no such thing as an old-fashioned hair stylist or barber. I still use roller sets to give hair volume because that works for me.

What works for you is what's best for you and you deserve a place that will make your techniques grow.

### Wisdom Key #27: Where there is no growth, there is no motivation

When your profession stops making you happy and turns into a job and just another thing you can do it's time to quit. All of us have points of frustration but that doesn't mean quit it means change your approach until you feel better about your situation. Go on a vacation somewhere, sometimes I run away to San Francisco by myself to go to the beach and think and pray and I feel one hundred percent better when I come back in the evening. Don't let your motivation get killed in winter weather when it's slow a lot of the time. Save during the busy times because slow times are coming!

I stay motivated through relaxation. If I can't steal away, everyone around me will know I need a break. What motivates you and how do you stay consistent in what you do? That's real wealth. Anything you love that you can stay consistent in is real wealth.

# Chapter Eight

## A Beauty Bar ™

**Est. 2:3- "Let the king appoint administrators in all the provinces of his kingdom, and have them gather all the beautiful young virgins to the citadel in Susa, into the harem, under the custody of Hegai, the king's eunuch, who is in charge of the women; and let <u>their beauty preparations be given to them.</u>**

Simple name for my baby right? The concept came from Queen Esther in the bible. God was not mentioned one time in that book but His works and movements are documented. People need a place to prepare for the King. The King of Glory, the King of your home (spouse) or just life in general. Everyone likes to feel their best and be given options to do so. Thus I give you A Beauty Bar™. Yep, this is the name of my salon! At one of my locations there is a two week waiting list to get in my chair. It was just a name for a long time before it manifested into the business I dreamed about as a little girl and I'm going to tell you what makes A Beauty Bar™ different:

1. **I came into ownership with GREED completely as a non-factor part of the A Beauty Bar™ equation!**
   a. You've only seen a little bit in this book of what I've gone through.
   b. I know what it's like to be in every aspect of this business from sweeping floors to dealing with difficult co-workers and customers and feeling robbed when I got my paycheck!
   c. I came into ownership with the mentality of service. I want people working with me to be better than me. I want you to go further, travel more and go higher than I've ever been! I want people working with me to be happy, not working for me to get more stuff.
2. **I have the mentality of not being in competition with anyone because no one does what I do like I do it.**
3. **I wish other CEO's would catch on that they have enough!**
   a. I remember working for a large corporate chain and nothing was ever enough! I made them over $150,000 in a year with some CEO's getting the tax breaks while I took home $15,000 where's the fairness in that? It was never ENOUGH!

**A Beauty Bar ™ has the concept that everything is fair across the board for everyone!**

- I don't do favorites, I don't do politics! I did that so everyone will stay "real" and honest with me. Snitching and constantly telling me every little thing wrong with everybody won't get you anywhere I find I deal with very little garbage from people if I don't listen to people's garbage in the first place.
- I don't leave broken things around in my businesses longer than five days! **Broken things are my pet peeve!** Nothing says low budget more than a leaky shampoo bowl, a broken dryer that doesn't blow out hot air, chipped and peeling paint on walls, out of service bathrooms and broken appliances. I've worked in so many places that function in dysfunction! If a round brush breaks on me, I throw it away! **IT IS SO ANNOYING TO**

Chapter Eight:

A Beauty Bar

**WORK FOR SOMEONE THAT FORCES PEOPLE TO WORK WITH THEIR BROKEN EQUIPMENT!** If you don't know anyone who fixes hydraulic chairs you need to find someone! Every business owner needs to have four people on speed dial:

1. Your attorney- for obvious reasons.
2. Your plumber
3. Your business handyman- to fix broken equipment.
4. Whoever is next in charge when the owner isn't available to answer questions.

- I teach people my techniques so I can leave a client and someone else can continue with them and I can jump back in where they left off. I love a well-oiled Beauty machine!
- If I'm busy I pass clients along to my co-workers. I can't do everyone and I believe there is enough for everyone!
- I allow my coworkers to use retail to supplement their income. They get 25-40% commission selling my retail. I own my product lines and I say what it sells for and I am not a greedy woman. Sometimes services are slow on rare occasions but the retail part of my business is busy so everyone sells and everyone gets credit.
- Businesses wouldn't see so much turnover if they learned how to be more fair.

Wisdom key #29 is for business owners and if you aspire to be one someday, you may appreciate my sound advice and questions:

## Wisdom Key #29: Absorb sound advice!

1. **Why hire people that don't make the cut?**
    a.) Maybe a candidate can cut hair but has bad customer service so why hire them?
    b.) Maybe a candidate has good customer service but low productivity. A Barber is not going to make much money taking forty minutes for one haircut!
   b. **Why hire someone who won't make the cut if you're not willing to train?**
    a.) It's fine to take people in that just graduated beauty school because every student is at their own level. If you're not willing to invest in a person's growth let them go somewhere else to get training so they can come back and try again.
2. **Why hire people you can't afford?**
    a. All companies go through trials and the first thing to consider when cutting costs sometimes means cutting payroll. I have watched companies cause people to struggle in an effort to get out of paying people unemployment, they force people to quit because no one can live on minimum wage and less than twenty hours a week. It would be better all the way around just to let people go.
    b. When you start a new beauty employee don't take on someone else in an effort to build your business quickly. Wait until the last person you hired is built a little or you could be asking for a conflict when it comes to new customers! The more new people you take on at once, the more struggle it will be for them to fill all of

their appointment books. On the other hand if you have the clientele to support new people- the more the merrier!

## Wisdom Key #30: Don't play games with people!

I don't mean to be offensive but you see I come from a place of experience but I have never stolen or manipulated anyone or anything to get an advance over people.

If there' something you can't deliver on or a promise you can't keep it's better to be upfront with people than to deceive them. If people can't trust your character, they won't trust your business either!

If there's one thing I hate and absolutely can't stand because it's happened so many times is being lied to my face! The second I feel I am being taken advantage of I will never again do anything for that person. A liar is always found out eventually! When they are their entire history and everything they've said is doubted. Why go through all that? Just tell the truth!

People that know me know I carry around a big red book. It's an organizer and I write down phone conversations, email notes etc. I can go back to the year 2005 and recall a conversation because you never know when you need to prove what you've been told! Some may think it's anal but I call it "proof".

## Wisdom Key #31: Communication!

A question should not have a million different answers! If a client calls over the phone and is quoted a price and gets to your place of work and their technician quotes them something different there is a problem! A communication problem. Please do yourself and everyone around you a favor and communicate and make sure they communicate with you as well.

### Don't expect people to follow guidelines you have not made clear!

When I worked for the barber college I was constantly blamed for not being psychic! The lack of communication made it impossible for me to do my job the way it should have been done. For example, I would not lie to the students about anything! But I was asked too! "Just tell them their kits were back ordered." I'm not saying that when they're sitting in your office and you're hanging on to them until their tuition payment comes through from the government! Lying was never in my job deception and I was never paid enough to compromise...the people I worked for knew who I really am and God is not pleased with deception! If I knew how much deception was involved I wouldn't have taken the job in the first place!

Let me make it very clear when I say there is no perfect place of work but there is a perfect place you can be in that makes your career work. At A Beauty Bar™ I make it my own personal best to make sure everyone working with me is all on the same page.

Chapter Eight:

A Beauty Bar

When welcomed on board everyone received the same operations manual, everyone received the same welcome gifts and everyone is taught A Beauty Bar™ culture. It has happened that a person that began with us didn't like our culture and rather hold them back I released them to explore other opportunities. I gave them time, I didn't play any games, we talked about what they really wanted to do and that was a choice best for them and A Beauty Bar™- this was not a personal decision. When that person gets more color training and builds up their speed I will welcome them back with open arms! No harm done.

## Wisdom Key #32: Please realize it only takes one bad review to ruin what you've worked for!

I don't hire people with nasty bad attitudes! They can try to hide it but sooner or later how a person really is shows. One thing I will not tolerate is someone making me look bad after everything I've fought and won for. If someone's bad habits or negativity (which is very contagious) starts a brush fire among the morale in my places of business that person would be cut quickly. I give people the freedom to be who they are but if a person comes to work and corrupts everyone there- I have a zero tolerance policy that everyone is aware of coming in!

## Wisdom Key #33: Learn how to forgive!

Some people are young and need time to mature. Some people have a bad day and bring it with them to your business. People go through things, you and I go through things that is life! Learn to let stupid petty things go! Someone parked in my parking space! So what! Someone messed up the appointments! Work it out so we can get through the day! It's best not to harp over things that are said and done. Some people don't like each other, let's talk about it and resolve it as grown people and if there is no resolution, so be it and we can all go our separate ways!

I know this is a little unorthodox but I love every single person I work with! I do my best to keep my people and sometimes things change but the people with me have been with me since the beginning. A Beauty Bar™ has very little turn over- ever! Thank God! I've had people stop to continue college, one had a baby and another moved away. There were no falling outs, we planned their exits together and everyone is welcome back any time!

### People make mistakes!

Everyone working with me has messed up inventory, sales, scheduling, phone calls, breaks communication etc! We all are human! Money has been misplaced but never stolen thank God. When you pay your people enough they don't steal from you and plus the people working with me are all afraid to go to jail!

## No matter what business you have anywhere

## You do not own people!

At A Beauty Bar™ people don't owe me anything. I don't owe people anything either. Yes I train, I give and educate and if people walk away after I invested so much in them, that decision is entirely up to them.

This is a problem I had to explain to the Barber College owner that I worked for is that he had a problem when he found out I had another full time job and didn't tell him. I explained it was because I didn't trust him. He didn't pay me enough so I found an additional company that would. He was a kid with control issues. Anything anyone does outside of my business is their business! I don't care as long as what they're doing does not affect me, I don't care! I have worked at more than one salon at a time and I didn't see it as a conflict of interest when the salons are 30 miles away from each other! I had to lovingly correct the kid and bring him back down to earth because I don't belong to anyone but Jesus Christ and if he was that concerned about it, he should have had me sign an anti-conflict of interest contract or something!

**All schools are not the boogey man in disguise!**

If I came out of school with all of my limbs still intact you can too! I make it my own personal effort to be upfront and honest with you when I say "yes all schools are a mess because they're run by people who are as human as you and I!" People make mistakes but it's you're responsibility to make your needs known. If you're beginning school the likelihood of it being owned by someone in your profession is unlikely. Even if they are licensed they may have been so through their own institution which is not illegal as long as they have supporting documentation and who's to say that documentation was earned honestly?

## A Beauty Bar Academy™

The best way I have been given the opportunity to provide a school that gives others everything I didn't have in a school experience. A.B.B.A. was not stumbled upon by accident. My slogan and mission for the academy is "Educational Excellence!" And this must live up to my Father's name. I don't just teach, I instruct life and career coaching and I don't leave my students to entertain themselves with today's technology, they know they are here to work! From the time a client comes through the door they are greeted with water, coffee, our ABB Newsletter (free to take home) and they are informed when their professional will be with them. My school is designed like a salon. Wide open space, and not a hen house full of cackling women. The environment is full of soothing instrumental jazz and the client is guided through our nail and skincare departments and given their service and add-ons and then escorted to the front and rebooked.

Did I mention this is all by apprenticeship? That's right, if you're a part of a two year long program, your skills hopefully will be mastered to perfection so the students are prepared for a career!

# A WORD FOR THE SCHOOL OWNER

Chapter Eight:

A Beauty Bar

Please stop trying to be everyone's friend! Students want to learn, they like structure and believe it or not they like when we stick to discipline and rules! I have a strict respect culture in my businesses and I am careful not to violate anyone's boundaries if others are careful not to disrespect mine. My door is always open and I always try to listen and adhere to the needs of my students as well as staff.

Please don't let people disrespect your school by letting them get away with spitting on the opportunities you have afforded them by assisting them with getting their license. Don't let people break your own rules! Don't force your instructors to compromise!

Schools today are quicker to fire good instructors before they release a student. Not so at A.B.B.A! Also I have never lost or kicked out a student because just don't let anyone enroll. Every applicant has to read this book and take a test before we interview and how they score and how they interview determines whether they become a student or not. It has happened during an interview people find this business is not a get rich quick scheme and it's okay, we're just not right for each other. I look out for everyone's best interest and if a person doesn't have drive or are not teachable, I'm sorry this is not for you! I'm not afraid of losing money! I've lost money before and God restored it! I said it before and I'll say it again, there is more to life than money and stuff. I'd rather have a quality small business than have a fortune 500 company with cancer! Think about it!

Chapter Eight:

A Beauty Bar

## Chapter 9:

## P.R.O™

**2 Cor. 2:9,10- Now He who provides seed for the sower and bread for food will provide and multiply your seed for sowing [that is, your resources] and increase the harvest of your righteousness [which shows itself in active goodness, kindness, and love].**

I developed Professional Resource Organization™ (P.R.O) for guess who? You and I. At the beginning of 2015 I wanted a resource available to help people avoid my experience. My role in this company is "Owner and Placement Expert". The number one complaint I receive from business owners is about staffing. I like to think P.R.O is the missing link in the beauty industry chain.

P.R.O has been established to place people in the workplace they need in order to grow. If you come to me as a newly licensed person I don't refer you, I place you. I network so you don't have too.

Employment assistance is like telling you "this place is hiring". How do you know this place is good for you? How do you know they need you as much as you need them? Who takes out your guess work for you? P.R.O does! Likewise if you're a beauty employer (shop owner) and need certain excellent staff, you come to me and we determine your needs and I bring you all the candidates you need! I make it my effort to make my services affordable in installments because I have been there and done that!

**And I don't stop there!**

I offer packages of advertisement and I will do my best to get you the exposure you need! If you need more clients I can help you build and give you the branding tools you need to help make your dreams come true without working hard; I help you work smart! I have made companies hundreds of thousands of dollars with techniques I can't share with you here but if you fill out an assessment on my website www.provizion.org and join my free online beauty community I promise it can be life changing for you!

I have a 100% success rate of people staying with their place of business and people loving their new recruits!

Also, a huge part of my culture at P.R.O™ is advertisement:

**Wisdom Key #34:**

Chapter Nine:

P.R.O

Professional Resource Organization

## Advertise, Advertise, Advertise!

I can't say it enough! No matter where you are, from the time you're in school to the time you're a seasoned professional you must exercise every avenue of advertisement within your budget.

Whatever practice you're in whether makeup artist, cosmo or barber – whatever everyone with hair and skin needs your business card! There is never a time I don't have 1,000 business cards on me at any one time. In my mind everyone needs what I have and the same is true for you!

## Everyone needs what you have!

Word of mouth is one thing but you don't have time to wait for recommendations from your friends because nine times out of ten people will not pass your information along according to your needs. If you need clients right now you must pursue people like you need air!

I never sit clients in my chair and not take the opportunity for them to fill out a client card! I need their name (first and last), phone number, address, email and birthday (because I give gifts and send cards for birthdays).

Utilizing social media is something anyone can use with their easy to use tools therefore it is essential that every beauty professional have a smart phone! It is so important to stay current with the times!

Make a quick before and after video and upload it a few times a day. See if within a week if your popularity doesn't increase. Why does this method work? Because the public is visually stimulated.

## Every beauty professional should have a website!

It doesn't take that long to post pictures and talk about yourself online! Some sites are free and allow you to do email blasts and book appointments online.

## Wisdom Key #35:

## You must make a connection!

It's one thing to collect information and keep in contact online and through the mail but there is nothing like genuine connection. When my regular clients come in

Chapter Nine:

P.R.O

Professional Resource Organization

everyone knows their name! We ask about our clients' children, spouse, who was in the hospital? How are they doing? We extend condolences and have baby showers. We have bachelorette parties and fight nights, annual events, shows and sometimes we hang out and invite the family for bowling. We stay connected with each other and have real fun!

Making a connection involves very little creativity. Many barbers that I've worked with share great stories and get us all laughing and laughter always connects people!

You don't have to be a comedian to show people how they can enjoy you. Sometimes while I do a pedicure I just listen to my clients get whatever they need too off their chest. Some have cried on my shoulders and some have been with me for years and we get emotional together.

There was a client I had that lost her granddaughter to s.i.d.s and I did her hair for the funeral. We both cried. She told me that she had shoes bigger than her grand babies' casket. People need you more than you know. I was able to make my client laugh and I changed subjects to help lighten her emotionally.

When clients feel better it helps the grieving process. I also work with elderly client as well and they go through depression the majority of the time. They come by just to talk to us. Everyone needs human touch.

Well now you know my big secret (which really isn't a secret at all) how I attaint my clientele. When I provide service for anyone I make them look the way I would want my hair, nails, eye brows, makeup or what ever to look. If there is something I don't have enough adequate time, then I refer my client to someone else. Referring is a form of good advertisement.

I can't do haircut designs! I have barbers to do that! They cut portraits, freestyle designs etc. I never learned haircut designs because I don't have to- I have the option to refer. There' nothing wrong if you don't specialize in something; sending a client somewhere else!

## Wisdom Key #36: You will get out of your career exactly what you put into it

Chapter Nine:

P.R.O

Professional Resource Organization

It isn't wise to invest a lot into things that depreciate. Don't be a work-a-holic to put rims on your car or invest in studio sound equipment and you can't sing so when it comes time to retire all you realize is you're too old to hold clippers and there's nothing to fall back on!

If you're working hard in your business don't you deserve to own your own property? Think about it…houses don't usually depreciate and home ownership can do wonders for your credit then you can have whatever you want! You can use your house to send your kids to college, buy and own cars! Don't live your life making payments…own something!

The same way you should have an entrance plan into this business is the same way you need to develop an exit plan. How do you want to finish your career? Do you want to end up with you and your spouse on a beach on an island drinking matai's or do you want to change careers down the line?

**As you made a plan to come in, you must have a plan to go out!**

# Chapter 10:

## My love letter I leave to you

**2 Cor. 2:4- I wrote that letter in great anguish with a troubled heart and many tears. I didn't want to grieve you, but I wanted to let you know how much love I have for you.**

I know this is an odd way to conclude a book but I have given you the best information I can with my life's experience.

I am not perfect, having a jaded attitude as if someone owed me something in the beginning of my career was the biggest mistake I made when I could have been learning more from my experience. At times I had such a victim mentality as if something were wrong with everyone else and everyone else was always doing something wrong to me…it was me too.

**Never be afraid to take responsibility because you were wrong.**

My biggest challenge working with students was they never thought they earned the consequences that they did. No one rewards a poor performance. Someone please let me know when awards are given to the worst athletes and the most inconsistent people! There are none!

Going forward the best advice I can give you is to be patient because success doesn't happen overnight. Have fun and don't forget where you came from. Be honest and law abiding so authority and State Board won't devour you!

I wrote this book because there is no reason to go through all you go through in school and getting licensed not to be successful or use your skills after you're license because you didn't know completely what you were getting into.

## Chapter Ten:

### My love letter I leave to you!

When I first started beauty school I was so sweet. By the third year into my career I started to get bitter because it didn't look like my efforts were being rewarded. By the time I moved to Georgia and got taken advantage of a few times I became hardened. I was hardened to the fact I taught myself to have no emotion. If you don't expect anything you can't be disappointed right? If I got fired, I had no emotion, no tears, I was too arrogant for that.

Cutting my emotions off is not a bad thing when done correctly. No matter what anyone tells me be it good or bad I am not moved!

Don't let people control your thoughts so much that they take you to another level and cause you to come out of your character.

If I would have slowed down and listened peoples motives would have been exposed to me and I wouldn't have made some choices that I did. If I wouldn't have made it about the money but the quality I would have gone into business for myself with less fear. Looking back I've worked for a lot of crooks that meant my harm but God turned it all around for my good.

Through this industry I have traveled and gone places I had never dreamed. I've met amazing people and I pray the same for you if that is your desire.

## Don't let your life be a reflection of people's opinion!

One thing I don't tolerate is people telling me where they think I should be. I would look at them and think "why are you speaking on something you know nothing about...like what God told me!" He told me from the beginning what I am doing will make me rich and what I do for others will last as long as the earth remains!

## Chapter Ten:

### My love letter I leave to you!

People have told me "I think a full service salon would be better for you." Or "I think working in this place or that place would be good for you". If you're not paying my bills or know my goals or me for that instance, why are you telling me where I should go? You should never consider the opinions of people that don't have your best interest at heart

Don't take on things you're not ready for. Don't jump into something because it looks good but you don't have all the details you need.

Test people's intentions! How do you do that? Give them time. As I said before a liar always gets found out and it takes time but sooner or later the truth always surfaces and you always have to pay attention.

If you get rejected, don't take it personal. Chalk it up to experience and move on. Whether you realize it or not even rejection can make you better. Through rejection you may come to find you dodged a major bullet!

Lastly, thank you for allowing me to share my journey with you. I pray I shared some wisdom that you can utilize to make your career a great one.

Please don't ever compromise your integrity or your quality because those things give you a good name and that's all any of us really have. Integrity is doing what's right when you think no one is looking. If someone can't be trusted privately, they can't be trusted openly.

The most valuable ability you can have in this life is love.

## 1 Cor. 13:4-7

Love is patient, love is kind. Love is not jealous or boastful or proud or rude. It does not demand its own way. It is not irritable,

**Chapter Ten:**

**My love letter I leave to you!**

and it keeps no recur of being wronged. It does not rejoice about injustice but rejoices whenever the truth wins out. **Love never gives up, never loses faith, is always hopeful and endures through every circumstance.**

**Please know in all things you are loved by an Almighty God and to God and the Lord Jesus Christ be all the glory, honor and praise! Amen!**

## About the author

La'Sandra Easley is a California native that began her career in Cosmetology at the age of 15. With a large body of work behind her she has contributed great assets to her brand such as :

After her return to California La'Sandra established "New Anointing" bath and body care line. Each unit of New Anointing bath and body care contains anointing oil from Israel hence the name "New Anointing".

In the end of 2013 La'Sandra developed the custom blending concepts of "A Beauty Bar" under the firm belief that "nothing we use on our clients should come from the same bottle."

In 2014 La'Sandra developed the line that barbers love to use and their clients adore by the name of "DoMenion" which is an all-natural and organic skincare line exclusively for men and only available to professional barbers!

La'Sandra developed the concept of professional resource organization because of the majority of beauty businesses and barbershops are revolving doors and p.r.o provides staffing options for businesses and provides options for professionals to find the perfect place to work!

www.ingramcontent.com/pod-product-compliance
Lightning Source LLC
Chambersburg PA
CBHW021923170526
45157CB00005B/2167